Smooth Sailing

Columbus, OH

The **McGraw·Hill** Companies

Revised under the direction of the Dolch Family Trust.

SRAonline.com

 SRA

Send all inquiries to:
SRA/McGraw-Hill
8787 Orion Place
Columbus, OH 43240-4027

Printed in the United States of America.

ISBN 0-07-603205-1

1 2 3 4 5 6 7 8 9 QPD 12 11 10 09 08 07 06 05 04

The McGraw-Hill Companies

Table of Contents

Giant Squids!

On a warm summer night a big boat sat in the deep dark waters of a large lake. All the people on the boat were sleeping. All but one, that is.

David was in his bed, but he was far from sleeping. He kept thinking about giant squids. Grandpa had told David and Phil about the squids right before it was time for bed. The giant squids sounded so scary that David was afraid he would never sleep on this boat or on any boat again.

This was Grandpa's boat. Grandpa had been all around the world on it. And before Grandpa got this boat, he had worked on big ships and small ships. Grandpa knew a lot about boats and the sea.

As Grandpa went around the world, he would see many kinds of fish and animals. So he knew a lot about the fish and animals that live in the world's seas.

Now that David was almost ten, his mother had let him and his big brother Phil stay with Grandpa for part of the summer. Grandpa, David, and Phil fished every day on the boat. On some days they would catch a lot of fish. On other days they would not catch any. But they always had fun.

David had been happy on the boat with Grandpa until they had talked about the scary giant squids. Grandpa's talk about giant squids was creepy. David already knew a little about squids. He had learned about squids in school last year.

A squid, David knew, has ten arms, two of which are very long. It has a strong beak like a bird. It also has two big eyes. Even in school, David thought a squid was a scary looking animal!

And David knew what a squid does with all those arms. A squid uses its arms to catch and hold fish and other sea animals. Part of the squid's arms stick right to the fish or animal. That is really creepy!

A squid does another creepy thing. It changes its color to hide in the water and on the bottom of the sea. A fish does not see a squid until the squid reaches out and surprises it.

The good thing is that most squids are small. But Grandpa did not tell David and Phil about small squids. Grandpa told them about scary, creepy giant squids! No wonder David could not sleep.

David did not want to think about what Grandpa had said. But as David lay on the bed in the boat, he could not help it. It was like a picture in his head that he saw again and again.

That morning David, Grandpa, and Phil had fished a lot. Grandpa had showed David and Phil how to clean all the fish they got. Then they had cooked the fish for dinner. The fish had tasted so good!

Then David, Grandpa, and Phil sat on the deck of the boat as the sun set. They were talking about fish and sea animals. Grandpa had seen many of them as he went around the world.

"I have seen all kinds of sea animals, but I have never seen a giant squid. I would still like to see a giant squid," Grandpa had said.

"A giant squid?" Phil asked. "How big is a giant squid?"

"Well, a live giant squid has never been found, so no one knows for sure. But I have heard that giant squids can be as long as a school bus or two," said Grandpa.

"As long as a school bus or two!" said David. "Giant squids must be monsters!"

Grandpa said. "That is what sailors said hundreds of years ago. In the old days when sailors would talk about sea monsters, they would often mean giant squids."

"They would?" David asked.

"Yes. The sailors would tell about sea monsters with long arms. They said the monsters would come out of the sea and use their long, long arms to reach out and take small ships."

"Like this one?" Phil asked.

"Oh no," said Grandpa. "This boat is not as big as those old ships."

Phil and David looked at each other. David did not like hearing that at all.

Grandpa told them more. "A giant squid's beak is so strong it can break big chains. Its eyes are large too. No animal on Earth has eyes as big as those of a giant squid."

"What does a giant squid eat?" asked David.

"Just like other squids, it eats fish and other sea animals," said Grandpa. "But the giant squid can eat big fish and big sea animals."

"Big animals such as whales?" asked Phil.

"Giant squids can eat whales, but whales can also eat giant squids," said Grandpa. "Some whales and giant squids have big fights. Whales win most often."

Now as he lay in bed, David was thinking and thinking. Giant squids as long as a school bus or two!

Ten long arms! Strong beaks! David could not believe that Grandpa and Phil were sleeping. How could they sleep when there could be a creepy, scary giant squid in the water under the boat right now?

Just then, David heard a creepy sound deep under the boat. He sat up in bed. "What was that?" he thought. "Was it a giant squid? Was it the long arm of a giant squid starting to wind around the boat?"

David did not know what to do. Should he get up? If there was a giant squid under the boat, just one of its long arms could reach out and take a boy like David. But David could not just stay there in bed. He had to find out what the noise was.

David got up and walked out on the deck of the boat. It was very dark. The air was warm, but David was feeling a bit cold. He knew it was because he was afraid.

As David stood on the deck, he could not see anything at first. But he could still hear the noise. David walked to the side of the boat and looked down into the deep dark water. He did not see anything. But he still heard the noise under the boat. Was it a giant squid?

Then David heard another noise behind him. Something was moving on the deck! It was moving across the deck to him. Was it the arm of the giant squid moving across the deck to get him?

David was afraid. He started to turn around when he heard, "David?"

It was Grandpa. He had been walking across the deck. It was not a giant squid's arm on the deck reaching out for David. "David, I thought I heard you out here. You are not sleeping?"

"I could not sleep because I have been thinking," said David. Then he heard the noise under the boat again. "What is that noise, Grandpa?"

"It is the chain from the anchor against the side of the boat, David," said Grandpa.

"The anchor," David said. "Oh, I should have thought of that."

"Did the noise from the anchor wake you up?" asked Grandpa.

"No, Grandpa, I could not sleep," said David.

Grandpa looked at David. He could tell David was thinking about something. Grandpa said, "Our talk about giant squids must have made you a bit afraid."

"A little," said David.

"Well, it is true that giants squids can be scary to think about it," said Grandpa.

"Yes, I don't like to think about them," said David.

"I am glad you told me," said Grandpa. "I did not mean to tell you something scary. David, giant squids live deep in the ocean. We are on a lake. It is a big lake, but there are no squids here."

David laughed. "You mean I did not even have to be afraid?" he asked.

"No, you did not," said Grandpa.

David laughed again. "Great, now I can sleep," he said. "Thanks, Grandpa."

"Good night, David," said Grandpa.

Rescue at Sea

Sarah and Jesse were doing what they often did in the morning. They were climbing up the steps in the lighthouse.

The lighthouse stood high above a spot of land that reached far out into the sea. Giant waves hit the rocks on three sides of the lighthouse.

This morning the sounds of the sea, wind, and birds filled the air. The bright sun made the lighthouse look as white as the two or three clouds in the blue sky above it.

Every five seconds, a very bright light would flash at the top of the lighthouse. Even in the bright morning sky, the flash could be seen from miles and miles away at sea. The flash told sailors that land was near. It told sailors to be careful of rocks and high waves near the land. Every day the flash of the light from the lighthouse helped save ships and sailors from the rocks and the waves.

If Sarah and Jesse looked out the window on the way up the steps, they would see a small red-and-white house. It was at the foot of the lighthouse. A door in the house opened right into the bottom of the lighthouse. The girls lived in the house with their mother, father, and baby brother, Robert.

If the girls looked out the window, they would also see a garden and lots of green grass around the house. A path made of stones went from the house to the road. The road went to town, which was several miles from the lighthouse where the family lived.

Sarah and Jesse were glad they lived in the lighthouse. It was a lot of fun. They would often run and play on the grass around the house.

But Sarah and Jesse had much work to do, so they did not often play in the morning. In the morning the girls did what everyone who lived in a lighthouse did. They worked hard to make sure the light in the lighthouse kept sailors and ships away from the rocks and high waves.

Sarah and Jesse's father was the lighthouse keeper. The keeper made sure the flash of the lighthouse never stopped. The keeper made sure ships stayed away from the rocks and high waves.

Most mornings Sarah and Jesse did what they were doing now—climbing up the steps. It was a long climb. There were almost two hundred steps to the top. Sarah and Jesse knew each step. They counted them every morning. The girls had strong legs. Most people who live and work in lighthouses have strong legs.

At the top of the steps was a room with windows on every side. In the middle of the room was a big light. The flash of this light was what sailors saw from far away.

But the girls knew that it was not the light that flashed. The light just turned around on a machine. The turning of the light on the machine looked like a flash from far away. When the sailors saw the flash, they knew they had to be careful not to run their ships into the rocks.

When the girls got to the room at the top of the steps, they did not even stop to rest. Their father had been up there already. He had looked at the machine and the light. He made sure both were working well.

He had also brought up two buckets of water. Their father was very strong. The buckets were for the girls to use to wash the windows. Right away, the girls started to work. The water in the buckets was warm. The hot sun kept everything in the room warm.

As Sarah and Jesse washed the windows, they could see far across the sea. A long way away, they could make out two or three big ships.

Sarah and Jesse knew those ships could see the flash from the lighthouse's big light. They knew the ships would stay away from the rocks. Knowing that the sailors on the ships could see the light made the girls feel good. They knew what they were doing was important because it helped many people.

As they worked, Jesse stopped to look out the window. "Look, Sarah, in the waves over there. What is it?" asked Jesse.

At first Sarah did not see anything. Then she saw what Jesse saw. "It is a small boat with a sail, and it is too close to the rocks! The boat is going to hit the rocks. The people in the boat are in trouble!"

The girls looked out for one more second. Then the girls looked at each other. They knew what they had to do.

A bell sat on the floor in the room at the top of the lighthouse. Sarah said, "Jesse, get the bell." Jesse picked up the bell and started ringing it. The ringing would tell Father and Mother a boat was in trouble.

Then the girls ran down the steps to the house. Sarah went first, and she ran fast. As she neared the bottom of the steps, Father yelled up, "Sarah, what is the trouble?"

"A small boat is near the north rocks. It is in trouble!" yelled Sarah as she kept climbing down the steps.

"You know what to do," Father yelled back up. As he said those words, he ran out the door of the house. Mother ran after him.

Sarah ran to where Robert sat on the floor. The girls would stay there to care for Robert until Mother and Father came back.

Jesse was down the steps now. She ran to the telephone. The girls knew they were to use the telephone to call when help was needed. Jesse picked up the telephone and called some people in town.

Sarah listened. Jesse told the people in town that a boat was in trouble and their mother and father were going out to try to get the people in the boat. The people in town said they were sending help.

Sarah and Jesse took Robert outside. The wind was starting to blow hard. The sisters could see Mother and Father in a big rowboat out on the sea. Mother and Father were rowing to the sailors in trouble. The girls could see Mother's red hair. They could see Father working hard to row the boat to where the sailors were.

The rowboat was moving fast. Both Mother and Father were strong and brave. But the waves were high, and they hid the rowboat now and then.

"I am afraid they will not make it to the small boat," said Jesse.

"They will. They are strong and brave," said Sarah. But she was afraid too.

Robert did not know what was wrong, but he knew his mother and father were not there. He started to cry. Sarah and Jesse looked at each other. They wanted to cry too.

Now the waves were so high that the girls could not see the rowboat at all. They just had to wait.

Sarah and Jesse had lived in the lighthouse for years. They knew sometimes it took a long time to row a big rowboat in high waves. They knew if Mother and Father made it out to the boat in trouble, it would take a long time to bring the sailors back to land.

The girls had also seen Mother and Father save people before, but not on a day like today when the waves were so high and the wind was so strong.

After watching the sea a little longer, Sarah and Jesse did what Mother and Father wanted them to do. They did not just stand and watch the sea anymore. The girls knew they could not do anything else to help Father and Mother. The girls would just have to wait. So they played with Robert, and they did a little work in the house.

After a while, Sarah and Jesse heard people from town on the road. They had come as fast as they could.

The people from town started to go out in rowboats to help Mother and Father. But then Jesse saw Father's rowboat in the sea.

"Look! There!" she yelled.

Sarah, Robert, and the others looked. The rowboat was on its way back! The waves were still high and hid it now and then, but the rowboat was close to the lighthouse!

In a little while the rowboat was closer. The girls saw Mother's red hair. They saw Father. They also saw four sailors in the rowboat.

Sarah and Jesse watched as the people helped pull the rowboat to land. Mother and Father had saved the sailors from the rocks and waves.

Island Dreams

The airplane looked like a large yellow-and-white bird moving across the sky. But it was not a bird, and it was not just any airplane. It was a seaplane.

The seaplane made small white waves in the water when it landed in the blue harbor of Key West near where Isabel's mother worked. The seaplane came across the harbor to pick up tourists who wanted to visit the islands of Dry Tortugas National Park.

Isabel often watched the seaplane land in the harbor. Every day tourists would wait at the harbor for the seaplane. She watched as the tourists climbed into the seaplane.

Isabel had read a book about Key West and the islands around it. She had a dream that one day she would be like those tourists and fly above the island of Key West and the ocean all around it. She wished she could fly to the islands of Dry Tortugas National Park.

Isabel's mother wanted Isabel's dream to come true. Mom often said, "One day, Isabel, you will go to the islands on a seaplane."

Isabel knew that sometimes dreams do come true, but flying in a seaplane cost a lot of money. She knew Mom worked hard at a job she liked, but she did not make a lot of money. Mom wanted to get another job so they would have more money. That was Mom's dream—to get a better paying job.

Mom loved to read. She read many, many books about Key West and the islands around it. She told Isabel about the seven islands of Dry Tortugas National Park.

Mom also read books that told all about the park. She knew the national park had an old fort, a lighthouse, pretty beaches, and many other things. Mom learned all about them. Mom and Isabel would often talk about what Mom had learned.

"Mom, you have learned so much from reading that you sound like you have already been to the fort, the lighthouse, and the beaches," Isabel said.

Mom said. "Well, I do like to read, and when your dream comes true, I want you to know all about the fort, the lighthouse, and the beaches at Dry Tortugas National Park." That made Isabel smile.

Mom came home from work early one Thursday night looking very excited.

"Isabel, I have a big surprise," said Mom.

"You got a new job?" asked Isabel.

"No, it is better than that," said Mom. "Some people at work had two tickets for a seaplane ride on Monday. They found out they cannot go."

"Yes," said Isabel. Now she knew why Mom was excited.

"They gave me the tickets, and I don't have to work this Monday! So early Monday morning you and I are going to use the tickets to fly on a seaplane to Dry Tortugas National Park!" said Mom.

Isabel was so excited. She could not believe it. Early Monday morning her dream would come true after all!

When she had time on Friday, Saturday, and Sunday, Mom read more about Dry Tortugas National Park. She also read a little book that told about the seaplane trip. It told what the seaplane would fly over, how long the trip would take, how fast the seaplane would fly, and more.

Mom and Isabel could hardly sleep Sunday night. Finally Monday morning came. Mom and Isabel were very excited about their trip. The seaplane would take them to Dry Tortugas National Park in the morning and bring them back to Key West in the evening. While they were at the park, Mom and Isabel could walk around the fort and the lighthouse.

The seaplane sat in the harbor. It bounced a bit when Mom and Isabel climbed in. The seaplane bounced in the water like a boat.

The seaplane had room for eight people and the pilot. Besides Mom and Isabel there were only two men in the plane. The pilot told Mom and Isabel that often the seaplane was not full on Mondays.

Mom and Isabel were in their seats. The motor on the seaplane started. The propeller started to turn. It was slow at first, then the propeller turned very fast. Over the sound of the motor, the pilot yelled, "Here we go!"

In seconds the seaplane was moving over the water in the harbor out to the open sea. The seaplane bounced up once and then again. It bounced once more and was out of the water and into the air!

"We are flying," yelled Isabel. She could not believe it! Just under her, she could see Key West. She could see the blue sea around the island.

In the air the propeller turned so fast that Isabel could see through it. The motor was not so loud now, so she and Mom could talk.

But Isabel did not talk. She just wanted to look out the window of the seaplane and listen to Mom talk about all the things Mom had learned. Isabel was glad to listen to Mom because Mom was a good storyteller. It made the trip even more fun.

Mom told Isabel many things about Key West and Dry Tortugas National Park. Mom had learned about the seaplane too. She told Isabel what kind of motor the seaplane had, how high it was flying, and more.

The pilot could not hear Mom, but the two men could. As Isabel turned around to look out all the seaplane's windows, she could tell the men were listening to every word Mom said.

At first Isabel did not think it was any big thing that the men were listening. Then she began to wonder about it. Who were these men, and why were they listening to Mom?

But Isabel did not wonder too long. There was too much to see, and Mom had too much to say.

The seaplane flew over a shipwreck. The shipwreck was in clear, blue water. Isabel could see the deck of the ship from the air. Mom told Isabel all about the shipwreck and why the water was so clear.

When the seaplane came to Dry Tortugas National Park, the pilot flew around the seven islands. Mom told Isabel a little about the fort and the lighthouse as the seaplane flew over them. It was clear that the two men were still listening to every word Mom said. As Mom talked, Isabel started to wonder about it again.

As the seaplane came close to land, it flew over the yellow beaches of Dry Tortugas National Park. Waves came up around the sides of the seaplane as it landed on the water.

Isabel was glad to visit the fort and the lighthouse. But she was also excited about the seaplane trip back to Key West. It was fun to fly!

As Mom and Isabel walked around Dry Tortugas National Park, Mom told Isabel story after story about the fort and the lighthouse. Each story Mom told made Isabel want to know more.

But every now and then, Isabel saw the two men from the seaplane. The men seemed to be following Mom and Isabel. They seemed to be listening to Mom again. This made Isabel wonder more than ever. What did the men want? And why were they following Mom and Isabel?

At the end of the day, it was time to fly back to Key West. When Mom and Isabel walked on the seaplane, the only other people on it were the two men!

"Mom," Isabel whispered. "Have those men been following us?"

"Yes, we were," said one of the men. He had heard Isabel!

"We should have told you," said the other man to Isabel. "We were following you today and listening to your mother talk about the trip."

"Why?" Mom asked.

"We own this seaplane," said the first man. "And we have been looking for someone to act as a guide. We are looking for someone who knows a lot about Key West and Dry Tortugas National Park."

"When we first heard you talk, we thought you might be a good guide," said the second man to Mom. "But we needed to listen to you more to make sure. We know now you would make a great guide."

"We will pay you very well to tell people about the seaplane, the trip, and Dry Tortugas National Park," said the first man.

"Would you like the job?" said the second man.

"Two dreams can come true today, Mom," said Isabel. "Say 'yes.'"

And Mom did!

A Submarine Adventure

The tourists sat in the submarine *Sea Search* and waited for their trip to begin. When most tourists come to Aruba, they know they can do many fun things. But most do not know they can ride in a real submarine!

Aruba is one of the many islands in the Caribbean. People from all over the world come to visit this beautiful island with its warm beaches and sun-filled towns. Some people love to fish. Some just want to rest in the sun. Others take tours.

People know they can take tours on boats, in airplanes, or on buses. Some people like to see Aruba on horseback or on bicycles. Touring on horses or on bicycles is a good way to see the land up close. The horses and bicycles can go to many places on the island buses cannot. But it is always a surprise to many tourists to learn that tours can take place on a submarine too. Submarine tours are quite an adventure because the tours take place underwater.

The tourists sat by *Sea Search*'s large windows. In a little while the tourists would be looking through these windows at the many wonders under the warm waters around Aruba.

Sea Search would be out in the ocean for a while. It would dive deep into the water. Then the tourists would see things most people never see.

The tourists heard *Sea Search*'s motor start. They heard *Sea Search*'s propeller turn.

"I am Captain Jair," said a man over the speakers. "I will do all I can to make your submarine ride a great adventure!"

The tourists listened to Captain Jair on the speakers as he told them about the dive. They were sure it would be an adventure.

Captain Jair said, "That is all for now. You will hear me again over the speakers soon. I will tell you about all the things you will be seeing in the ocean."

The submarine started to dive. The tourists were excited because their adventure had started! They looked out the windows. In seconds, the blue sky of Aruba turned into the blue waters of the Caribbean.

The small crew worked hard as the submarine went deeper. *Sea Search* was a fine machine, but even a fine submarine needs a careful crew to keep it out of danger.

Many things can go wrong when a submarine goes deep underwater. But Captain Jair had trained the crew well. They were trained to know what to do if there was trouble. Even better, he had trained the crew to make sure there would be almost no danger.

But the tourists did not think about danger. They were looking out the windows. The water turned a deeper blue as *Sea Search* went deeper into the ocean. The light of the bright sun still passed through the clear water.

The tourists could see fish of many colors. As *Sea Search* went deeper, Captain Jair came back over the speakers to tell them about the fish. Captain Jair had been the captain of *Sea Search* for a long time. He told the tourists many interesting things about the fish and the animals they saw.

Soon *Sea Search* passed over sponge beds full of color. Captain Jair spoke again. "A sponge is a sea animal without a head or arms. It looks like a plant. A sponge lives in just one spot, often on a rock. It cannot move from that spot. You know people wash with sponges. When we get back, you can buy a sponge to take home!"

As the journey went on, the tourists heard noises in the submarine as it made its way through the ocean. Captain Jair told the tourists not to worry. There was nothing wrong with the submarine. The sounds were just part of the journey as the submarine went into deeper water.

Captain Jair told the tourists the submarine was now going to a place that made most people feel a bit creepy—a shipwreck.

As *Sea Search* neared the shipwreck, the tourists looked hard out the window. The shipwreck was big. The tourists could see the ship's old wood deck, its anchor and propeller, and other parts of the ship.

"There is a secret about this shipwreck," said Captain Jair. "The secret is that this ship was sunk so tourists could dive down to see it. Don't worry, no one was hurt when this ship was sunk."

The tourists were glad to hear about the secret. Just then one of the tourists, a little boy, asked, "Captain Jair, is that a picnic basket in the water?"

"A picnic basket?" asked Captain Jair. He looked out a window at the picnic basket. It was there on the deck of the shipwreck. Was the picnic basket there so it would look like it was part of the shipwreck? Captain Jair did not think so. It did not look like an old basket that had been there for some time.

Captain Jair began to worry. He thought fast. He knew right away why the picnic basket was there. He hit a button by his chair.

The button turned on red warning lights that flashed all over the submarine. The red warning lights made the tourists afraid. The red warning lights made the crew take the submarine up, fast.

Captain Jair was on the speakers in seconds. "Please do not be afraid," he said. "We are not in danger, but other people on top of the ocean may be. We must go up to find out." The tourists looked out the window, but they were still a little afraid.

Captain Jair hit another button that made the periscope come up. He looked through the periscope as *Sea Search* climbed to the top of the water. The periscope let him see above the water. He saw another boat. Captain Jair now knew he was right to worry!

"Crew," yelled Captain Jair as *Sea Search* reached the top of the water. "Get ready to rescue some people."

The crew worked fast to get two small rowboats ready. The crew would use the rowboats to get the people and bring them back to *Sea Search*.

The tourists could now see what Captain Jair had seen through the periscope as they looked out the submarine windows. A boat had turned over in the water. Two people were hanging on to its side! They were in trouble. The people could not believe that a submarine had just come out of the ocean to rescue them!

"Captain Jair knew the picnic basket came from a boat above," said the little boy in *Sea Search*. "He knew it could mean the boat was in trouble. Now the crew will rescue those people."

The crew put the two small rowboats into the water and headed out to save the people. Captain Jair watched from the deck.

It did not take long for the rowboats to reach the people.

When the first rowboat got there, one of the crew asked, "Are you the only ones who were on this boat?"

"My father was on the boat," yelled one of the people. "I do not where he is now!"

One of the crew yelled back to the submarine, "One man is not here!"

"Look under the boat," yelled Captain Jair.

But as Captain Jair said that, he looked out across the water. In seconds he saw a red-and-green shirt. It was the man!

"Wait," yelled Captain Jair to the crew. "The man is over there." The man was in real trouble.

Captain Jair knew he had to act fast. He took off his shoes and shirt and jumped into the ocean. Captain Jair swam to the man in the red-and-green shirt.

Captain Jair swam fast through the waves to reach the man. The man's head looked like it was about to go under the water. Captain Jair swam very fast. Captain Jair got there just as the man was about to go under! Captain Jair kept the man from going under.

With his arm around the man, Captain Jair swam back to *Sea Search*. The crew in one of the rowboats came over to help him.

All three people from the boat were soon on the submarine with Captain Jair and the crew. All three were out of danger.

Captain Jair, the crew, and the three people walked down the steps from the submarine deck to where the tourists were.

The tourists cheered and cheered for brave Captain Jair and his crew. The three people cheered too. The submarine ride had been a real adventure!

The Cruise

Jorge came home from school to find his mother and father in the family room. They had excited, happy looks on their faces.

"Guess what, Jorge," said Dad with a smile.

Jorge did not know what to guess. But he knew Dad and Mom would laugh at a funny guess or two.

"We are buying a lighthouse on a faraway island?" asked Jorge.

"No, try again," Dad said as he laughed. Mom laughed too.

Jorge shut his eyes to make it look like he was thinking very hard. He was trying to think of another funny guess.

"I think I know," said Jorge. "I forgot to walk my elephant."

Both Mom and Dad laughed again.

"Well, I guess we will just have to tell you," said Dad. "We are all going on a trip together!"

"That sounds great," Jorge said. He was excited. His family had not gone on a vacation in some time.

"Where are we going?" Jorge asked.

Mom stood up and gave Jorge a brochure to look at. It was a brochure for a cruise ship. Jorge was really excited now.

"We are going on a cruise?" asked Jorge. "That will be so much fun. Are we going to take a cruise to Hawaii, or will it be to some other nice warm islands?"

Mom and Dad looked at each other. They pointed at the brochure. Jorge looked down at it again. "Alaskan Cruise Vacation," he read out loud.

Jorge looked through the brochure. It showed pictures of Alaska with snow on the ground. There were some pictures of people on the deck of a cruise ship, and they all had on big winter coats.

"We are going on a cruise vacation to Alaska?" asked Jorge. "But it is cold in Alaska."

"It will not be that cold, Jorge," said Dad. "We are going at the time of year when it is very nice in Alaska."

Jorge was happy to hear that. This was going to be a terrific vacation. Jorge did not know anyone who had been to Alaska. Jorge knew this would be a great trip.

"You are right, Dad," said Jorge. "It will be terrific. I will read the brochure and learn more about the cruise. May I take this to my room and look it over?"

"Sure," said Dad. "You may keep that one; your mother and I have another one right here."

Jorge picked up his school bag and took the brochure to his room. The picture on the front of the brochure was beautiful. It was a picture of a cruise ship in water with a terrific snow-covered mountain behind it.

Jorge looked again at the picture on the front of the brochure. Then he saw that it was not a mountain behind the ship at all. It was an iceberg!

Jorge had read a book about the *Titanic*. The book was the real story of the big cruise ship that started to cross the ocean a long time ago. The *Titanic* was out in the middle of the sea when it hit an iceberg. The book told about how the iceberg had made a great big hole right in the side of the ship.

Well, this was no good. Jorge did not like the thought of going on vacation on a ship that might run into an iceberg.

He looked through the rest of the brochure and looked at more pictures of the ship in water. There was another iceberg, and another!

Then Jorge heard Mom call him for dinner. He took the brochure and ran to the dinner table.

"Did you see this?" asked Jorge. He pointed at the iceberg behind the ship on the front of the brochure. Then he opened the brochure and pointed at other pictures that had icebergs in them.

"Those are icebergs, Jorge," said Mom. "The water is cold near Alaska. We will see seals and other animals resting on large icebergs."

"I want to see seals," said Jorge. "But what if we hit one of them?"

"Hit one of the seals?" asked Dad.

"No. What if we hit one of the icebergs?" said Jorge. He did not find what his father said very funny just then. "I don't think I will like being on a big boat in an ocean filled with icebergs. Can we change our vacation?"

"Now, Jorge," said Mom, "these ships cruise through the waters near Alaska all the time. They know how to stay away from icebergs."

Jorge and his parents talked about the trip over dinner. They told Jorge they could not change their vacation now. His parents had already sent money to the Alaskan Cruise Vacation people.

Jorge helped his parents clear the dinner table. Mom asked him about school and other things, but Jorge could not stop thinking about the cruise. He was worried about those icebergs.

"Are you worried about this trip, Jorge?" asked Dad.

"I guess so," said Jorge. "In the book about the *Titanic*, it says the iceberg made a great big hole right in the side of the boat. What if an iceberg does that to our ship?"

"Jorge, you should not be worried about that," said Dad. "These ships have machines and things to tell them if there is an iceberg near. The trip will be fine. You will have a great time."

The time for the vacation finally came. Jorge and his parents flew to Seattle, Washington, where they would get on the cruise ship. After waiting a bit in a building in the harbor, it was finally time to get on the ship.

Jorge and his parents made their way to their cabin. When they went inside the cabin, the first thing Jorge did was look out the cabin window at the harbor. He did not see any icebergs.

The ship set out, and the cruise began. It was a seven-day cruise. For the first two days, Jorge watched the ocean for icebergs. He did not see any. He still worried at first, but soon he forgot about icebergs. The ship had all kinds of terrific things for the family to do.

Just when he stopped thinking about the icebergs, Jorge looked out across the water. He stopped walking with his parents. He finally saw an iceberg!

"Dad!" yelled Jorge. "Dad! It is an iceberg! It is an iceberg."

"It is beautiful," said a woman's voice. But the voice was not his mother's. "It is a big one too," said the voice again. "And look, there are seals resting on it."

Jorge turned to find out whose voice this was. There in front of him stood the captain of the ship.

"Jorge is worried the ship will hit an iceberg," said Jorge's mother to the captain.

"That will not take place," said the captain. "We have radar."

"Oh, I know about radar." said Jorge.

"Right," she said. "And on the bottom of the ship, we send out a signal underwater. That signal tells us how close icebergs are. The signal and the radar protect us."

"Good," said Jorge.

"And there are airplanes that fly above these waters," said the captain. "They look for icebergs. They can tell if part of an iceberg is under the sea. The airplanes help protect us too."

The captain took Jorge and his parents up to the bridge of the ship. The bridge of a ship is where the captain can control the ship. The captain showed Jorge the radar.

"See that?" asked the captain. She pointed at a picture the radar showed. "That is an iceberg. Most of it is under the water, which is why we have to be careful. But the radar lets us know where the iceberg is so we can control how close we get to it."

"To protect us," said Jorge.

"Yes," she said. "A lot of people like to get close to icebergs because they like to see the animals that rest on them. And because we can control this ship so well, we can get close to them."

"Jorge, are you still worried that this ship will hit an iceberg?" asked Dad.

"No," said Jorge. "I think the captain has things well in hand with the radar. I cannot wait to see the seals resting on the icebergs."

Jorge's parents each flashed a smile. "Thanks, Captain," they said.

After that, Jorge had a terrific vacation!

Mystery in the Fog

Commander Stern started Stern's Whale-Watching Cruises back in 1954. And *Stern's Steamers* still take tourists out to sea to watch whales on most spring, summer, and fall days.

The cruises have not always been on the same *Stern's Steamer*. Right now *Stern's Steamer 5* leaves the harbor every morning. Several ships have been called *Stern's Steamer*. The number 5 means there have been five *Stern's Steamers*.

Today Amanda Stern and *Stern's Steamer 5* show tourists the wonder of whales just as Commander Isaiah Stern, her grandfather, did with the first *Stern's Steamer*.

When Commander Isaiah Stern started his cruises, ships then were not like today's ships. They did not have radar. And there were no Global Tracking Systems and satellites to help tell the ships where they were.

In 1954 no satellites of any kind were in the sky. Back then most people did not know what satellites were!

It did not matter to Commander Stern that he did not have radar or satellites. He was a good sailor. He knew how to go out to sea and come back to the harbor in Boston without much help—except for one time, that is.

Commander Stern started his whale-watching cruises because he needed money and because he loved the smell, feel, and sound of the sea. He also loved whales.

With each trip Commander Stern took, he grew to love the sea more and more. Tourists on *Stern's Steamer* could see how much he loved the sea. He loved it more than anything, except his family.

Commander Stern also learned more and more about the sea and about whales. He would look at a whale for a long time. He would try to remember things about that whale so he would know it if he saw it again.

Commander Stern gave names to many of the whales he saw each day. He named one Bart, another Cleo, and so on.

On most other whale-watching cruises, a ship's captain could tell tourists only what kind of whale they saw. No one could tell them the names of the whales, no one except Commander Stern!

Commander Stern was careful around whales. He loved them and never wanted to hurt them.

At times, when tourists asked Commander Stern to take *Stern's Steamer* very close to a whale, he would say that he could not because he did not want to put the whale in danger. Over time most whales seemed to know that Commander Stern loved them and would not put them in danger.

The whales learned to watch for *Stern's Steamer* because Commander Stern gave fish to the whales. The whales liked that. He also called each whale by name and talked to them as if they were friends. To Commander Stern, they were friends.

Many tourists came to Boston each year to go whale watching. The tourists would see several kinds of whales in these waters. Commander Stern would tell the tourists many things about the whales. He told them whales travel in schools. He would tell the tourists on his cruises that the whales came to that part of the ocean to find food before they headed south for the winter.

Sometimes the tourists would see the whales swim on their backs with both flippers sticking out of the water. And when the whales would stick their heads out of the water, the tourists could almost look them in the eyes! Then the whales would move their tails and hit the water with them. Sometimes the whales would get the tourists wet! The tourists loved to see the whales put on their show.

So when tourists wanted to go whale watching, they picked *Stern's Steamer*. On other whale-watching boats, they might not see any whales. But people always saw whales on *Stern's Steamer*.

That was good for Commander Stern because that was how he made money. And it was good that the whales seemed to love him too. That is, all but one. This whale was as big as any whale in the waters *Stern's Steamer* visited. She had a big scar under one eye, and she made a clicking noise. Commander Stern had never heard another whale clicking just like that.

At sea Commander Stern would often see this whale that seemed to not like him. At times he could see the scar under her eye and hear her clicking. But she never came too close to the ship.

Commander Stern wanted all the whales to love him. He was sad he could not make friends with that one big whale with the scar. But that was the way it was.

Besides, Commander Stern knew if he wanted to take a ship full of tourists into the Atlantic Ocean almost every day, he could not be worried about one whale who did not seem to like him. He had to do his best to help people have fun on the trip. He had to do his best to make sure people were not worried about the waves or the weather. He had to do his best to make sure the ship got back to the harbor safely.

Every day before *Stern's Steamer* left the harbor, Commander Stern read the weather report. If the weather report called for bad weather and Commander Stern thought his ship could not make it back safely, he would not take it out to sea.

Commander Stern did not want to put the tourists in danger. If he did not take the ship out, he would give money back to the tourists who had tickets.

One day in July 1957 Commander Stern had trouble bringing *Stern's Steamer* back into the harbor safely. That morning the weather report said the day would be clear and warm. It would be a great day to watch whales.

As *Stern's Steamer* left the harbor, Commander Stern did see a bit of fog out over the ocean. But there was often a little fog in the morning. When the sun got very bright, the fog would burn off or go away. It always did. This day, it did not.

The fog was still there as *Stern's Steamer* went far out onto the ocean. The fog was getting so heavy that it was hard to see. Soon Commander Stern could not even see the front of the ship!

But he could see the faces of the tourists on the ship. They looked afraid. They had come on *Stern's Steamer* to watch whales, not to be in danger!

As Commander Stern wondered what to do, a strong wind started to blow. Big waves rolled under the ship. *Stern's Steamer* bounced high.

Commander Stern had to act. He turned the ship left to where he thought the harbor was. But as he did, something pushed the ship hard the other way. Something made it turn to the right. Commander Stern was surprised. "What could be pushing the ship like that?" he wondered.

Then more big waves rolled under the ship, and it bounced again. Right away, something pushed the ship from behind. It pushed and pushed. Soon *Stern's Steamer* was moving fast.

Commander Stern could only wonder what was pushing the ship. He wondered if they were moving toward the harbor or out to the open sea.

Then Commander Stern heard a noise from the back of the ship. What was it? He had heard that sound before. Then he knew. It was clicking!

Commander Stern ran to the back of the ship and looked into the water. He saw a big whale with a scar under its eye. He could not believe it! It was the whale he thought did not like him.

But what was she doing? Was she helping the ship get to the harbor, or was she sending the ship out to sea?

Then one of the tourists on the ship yelled, "There it is! The harbor! We are going into the harbor!"

Soon the whale had safely pushed *Stern's Steamer* and the tourists into the quiet waters of the harbor. Commander Stern saw the whale jump in the harbor as she started to swim away. He called out to her, "Thank you, Amanda!"

That was a long time ago. And today Amanda Stern, *Stern's Steamer 5*, and several friendly whales still meet in the Atlantic Ocean almost every day.

Man Overboard!

Martin's job was to write for a newspaper. The newspaper sent him around the world. Martin would write articles about interesting places people could visit.

Martin had been to China, Russia, Japan, Iceland, Greenland, Spain, and Italy. He loved to write interesting articles about things like the Eiffel Tower and the Statue of Liberty. He also loved to write interesting articles about small towns like Dyersville, Iowa, and Jerome, Arizona.

Today Martin was on a ship in the South Pacific. The South Pacific is a part of the Pacific Ocean that has more than three thousand islands. Many of these three thousand islands are very, very small.

Martin's newspaper asked him to write articles about some islands in the South Pacific. He was going to visit Fiji, Tahiti, and Samoa. But his first stop was on the islands of Tonga, a small country with about one hundred thousand people.

Martin sat in his cabin on the ship. It was evening, and he was trying to read a book about the islands of Tonga. Whenever the newspaper sent him to a new place, Martin would get books about that place.

Martin read that Tonga has 170 islands. But people live on only about 45 of the islands. He read that tourists can visit only some of the islands. Tourists can do several things on the islands, such as whale watching and swimming. Martin wanted to learn as much about Tonga as he could. This helped him know which things he wanted to see and do when he got there.

But a storm had started to blow, and it was getting hard to read. The more the storm blew and blew, the more the ship bounced in the waves. Soon the words in the book bounced in front of Martin's eyes as well.

The captain and crew were on deck working hard to get the ship through the storm. The captain had told Martin he could stay in the cabin under the deck, out of the rain and wind.

Martin was not too afraid of the storm. The newspaper had sent him on many trips, and he had been through more than one storm. He was sure the captain and crew would get the ship safely through this one as well.

As Martin was reading, the lights in the cabin went out. The captain yelled down to Martin that the storm had knocked out the power on the ship.

"There are some matches in your night table," said the captain. "You can light the lantern down there until we get the power back on."

Martin found the matches in the table. He lit the lantern and put the matches in his pocket. The lantern gave his room some light, but it really was not enough to read by.

So Martin put on his coat, blew out the lantern, and went up to see how the captain and his crew were doing.

"Martin," said the captain, "we will not get the power back on until this storm lets up."

"That is fine, Captain," said Martin. "It was getting too hard to read down there."

Then a giant wave hit the side of the ship. Martin fell to the deck. As he did, the captain got hold of Martin's coat.

"Hang on, Martin, or you will be thrown overboard," said the captain. "And put on a life jacket!"

Martin put on a yellow life jacket over his coat. Just as he got it on, another giant wave hit the side of the ship. This time Martin was thrown overboard! In a flash, he was falling into the ocean.

The captain yelled, "Man overboard!"

The crew ran to help. In the dark waves, they could see Martin for a second or two in his yellow life jacket. But then he was gone. The captain yelled, "Get the lifeboat!"

As the crew ran to the lifeboat, the waves took Martin away from the ship.

Martin had hit the water hard when he fell and was knocked out. His life jacket kept his head above water. He began to drift far from the ship.

Right away some of crew got into the lifeboat in the ocean. They looked for Martin in the high waves.

Martin did not see or hear them. He just drifted and drifted away from the ship and the lifeboat.

On the ship, the captain ran to the radio to call for help. But the radio did not work. All the power on the ship was knocked out. As soon as the power was working, the captain would use the radio to call the Coast Guard.

Early the next morning the sun was out, and Martin was on a beach. He was on the sand in his yellow life jacket and his coat.

At first Martin did not know where he was. He remembered being on the deck of the ship and he remembered the life jacket. The last thing he remembered was that a giant wave hit the ship.

Martin knew he must have been thrown overboard. He did not know if others on the ship were thrown overboard too.

The life jacket the captain gave Martin had helped him stay above the water. If he had not had it on, he would not have drifted to this beach.

Martin took off his life jacket and coat. He looked around. The beach was long. He did not see any houses. Martin walked down the beach to see if there were people around.

On one side the beach ended at the bottom of a large cliff. So Martin turned and walked the other way. He walked and walked until he came to the other end of the beach. A big cliff was there too.

The beach had nothing but giant cliff walls all around it. Was Martin trapped here?

Martin walked along the bottom of the cliff walls to find some place he could climb up to look out. But he could not find a way out. Martin was trapped!

Martin needed to find water to drink. He walked along the bottom of the cliff walls looking for water. He looked carefully at the rocks. He thought he might find a small opening in the rocks where water might get through.

At last Martin did find a little water falling down the side of the cliff. He put his hands under it and took a drink. Then he put some on his face.

Now Martin was hungry. He had to look for food. Where could he find food if he was trapped on a beach? He thought he would have to catch some fish from the ocean. But how would he catch them? He would have to look for a stick and somehow make a point at one end.

"I am stranded on a deserted island," said Martin to no one.

Martin thought about the games he had played with his friends when he was a child. They would say, "If you were stranded on a deserted island, what would you want to have with you?"

Martin always said he would want a boat or an airplane. That sure would be nice right now, Martin thought. But then he remembered that one of his friends had said that if he were stranded on a deserted island, he would want to have matches.

Martin reached into his pocket and found the matches he used to light the lantern on the ship. They were wet, but Martin was glad to have them. He set them on the sand to dry.

Martin could use the matches and some wood on the beach to make a fire. The fire would be a signal for help to a ship in the ocean.

Martin heard a noise from the ocean. He turned and saw a tourist boat filled with people.

The boat came right up to the beach and onto the sand. The people got off the boat. The tourist boat was bringing people to the beach. Martin ran to the tourist guide and told him about the storm.

"We got a call about you," said the guide. "The captain of your ship was afraid you would never be found. He will be happy."

The guide then told Martin the tourist boat had come from the other side of the island. "The only way you can get to this side is by boat—or life jacket," he said.

Martin laughed. "What is the name of this island?" he asked.

"This is Kao," said the guide, "one of the islands of Tonga."

Martin laughed again. This would be one of his best articles ever.

A Brave Sea Swimmer

When Margaret sat down for breakfast, Father was already at the table. He had his newspaper in front of his face, just as he always did at breakfast. Margaret could see only the top of his head.

"Good morning, Margaret," Father said through the paper.

"Good morning, Father," said Margaret. "Any news?"

"Yes, there is," Father said with a smile as he set the paper on the table.

Father knew what Margaret was asking about. She wanted to know about Gertrude Ederle. All the girls in the family wanted to know about her. The boys did too.

"Well, did she do it? Did she swim the Channel?" asked Margaret.

The English Channel is a body of water between England and mainland Europe. To swim the 21 miles across the Channel was a dream of many top swimmers, but by 1926 only five swimmers had made it.

And all the swimmers who did were men. By 1926 no woman had made it across the Channel. Many people thought no woman would ever swim the English Channel.

Margaret knew that yesterday, August 6, 1926, a young American woman was going to try to swim the Channel. That young woman was Gertrude Ederle. Now Margaret wanted to know if she had done it. Did a woman swim across the English Channel?

"The morning newspaper tells all about Gertrude Ederle's effort," said Father.

"Well, did she do it?" asked Margaret.

"She made a terrific effort yesterday," said Father.

Margaret knew Father wanted to tell her everything the newspaper said. He was like that. But Margaret did not mind because Father told things very well.

"I will imagine it as you tell me, Father," she said.

"Good," said Father. "Two years ago, Gertrude Ederle did try to swim across the

Channel. But she did not make it then. With only seven miles to go, she was pulled from the ice-cold waters."

Margaret could imagine how Gertrude must have felt two years ago. She could imagine how sad it must have been to make such an effort and then not swim all the way.

"Gertrude then came back to America," Father said. "But she was still determined to swim the English Channel. She knew that hundreds of men had made the effort. But only five had made it all the way across the sea."

"Only five," thought Margaret. Gertrude would need to be very determined to make it all the way across.

"Gertrude was the only woman to try to swim the Channel. Many people would have said that trying was enough. But she wanted more. She was determined to be the first woman to swim all 21 miles," said Father.

Margaret knew that two years ago in the Olympics, Gertrude won a gold medal for swimming. She won other medals as well.

To have won an Olympic gold medal would have been enough for most people, but not for Gertrude. She still wanted to attempt another swim across the Channel.

Father said, "Now yesterday, when Gertrude made another attempt, the water in the Channel was ice cold. It also had strong currents."

Father went on. "The paper said these currents could make the attempt to swim across very hard. It would make the 21 miles feel like many more miles."

Margaret listened as Father spoke. All these things to worry about seemed to make this swim for Gertrude very hard. Just the currents would make it hard.

"Gertrude also had to worry about large boats and ships in the Channel," said Father.

In her mind, Margaret saw how bad it would be for Gertrude to swim into a big boat heading right at her in the Channel. Gertrude had many things to fear. Just thinking about them made Margaret afraid.

Father could see fear in Margaret's face. He always thought she should write books when she grew up. She would write well because she could imagine things like fear in a very real way.

"Gertrude would also have to watch out for jellyfish. Jellyfish sting and make it very hard to swim well. It is hard to worry about jellyfish when you are swimming through large waves," Father said.

Margaret thought that sounded hard too! She remembered that a friend of hers got a jellyfish sting. Her friend said it felt like her skin was on fire.

"Before she started swimming, Gertrude covered her body with oils," said Father. "These oils helped keep the ice-cold water from hurting her skin. The oils also helped make a jellyfish's sting not hurt as much."

Margaret had not thought before about how much Gertrude had to do just to get ready for the long swim.

"Yesterday at seven in the morning, Gertrude Ederle got into the water," said Father.

"She was not alone. In a boat by her side were her father, sister, and coach, Thomas Burgess. Reporters and friends were in another boat," said Father.

At first Margaret thought Gertrude might be alone in the Channel. Margaret was glad to hear that people in boats were near Gertrude as she made her swim. Margaret was also glad one of the people in the boats was Gertrude's father. Her father would try to make sure nothing bad took place.

"Gertrude started the long swim. She had to be careful not to swim too fast at first. That would make her tired too soon. If Gertrude felt she was going too fast, she would sing right in the water! Singing helped Gertrude slow down a bit," said Father. "She was not the only one to sing.

"The reporters and friends would sing with her too. That way, she knew she was not alone in the dark water."

Margaret was so happy to know that even the reporters who were following Gertrude wanted her to make it across the Channel.

"Several hours into the swim, Gertrude's left leg went numb," said Father. "The numb leg made it hard for her to kick in the water."

"Oh, no," thought Margaret. "She did not make it!"

"Gertrude's father wanted her to stop the swim. Her numb leg worried him," Father said. "If you were swimming the Channel, Margaret, I would have wanted you to stop too."

"Did Gertrude stop?" asked Margaret in a sad voice.

"No," said Father with a smile. "Gertrude knew she was hours into this swim, and she did not want to give up, so she stayed in the water and yelled to her father 'No! No!'

"Gertrude felt she did not have many more hours to go. So she kept singing and swimming. Gertrude's father knew she was determined."

Margaret was so happy Gertrude did not give up. It would be a great thing if a woman could swim the English Channel.

Then Father said, "After being in the water for many hours, Gertrude Ederle walked out of the water onto the shore at Kingsdown, England. She was tired and covered with the oils and dirt from the sea. But she did it! Hundreds of people were on the shore waiting for her. She did it! She was a hero."

Yes! Yes! Margaret jumped up and down. "Terrific! Gertrude is a hero!" she yelled.

Father laughed and said, "Gertrude Ederle is a hero! The people on the shore thought so, and now people all over the world know so."

"Father, do you think her father was angry when Gertrude's leg went numb and she would not stop swimming?" asked Margaret.

"No, I am sure he is very happy now and very proud," said Father. "Any father would be proud."

"I am proud of her too," said Margaret.

"And I have not even told you the best part," said Father.

"What?" asked Margaret.

"Not only was Gertrude Ederle the first woman to swim across the English Channel," said Father, "but she did it much faster than any of the five men before her. She was faster by more than two hours."

"Faster? Two hours faster!" yelled Margaret. "That means a woman can do anything!"

Father laughed and said, "I always knew that!"

Swimming with Whales

The sea near Hawaii is very quiet. The waves and wind don't kick up as much there as in other parts of the ocean. It is a special place, a place where many whales come.

A boat was moving through this part of the sea. Some of the men and women on the boat were scientists. The scientists and the crew were on a special journey. The scientists wanted to learn more about whales. But they wanted to do it in a special way that no one had ever done before. They wanted to swim in the ocean with whales!

When people first heard about what the scientists were going to attempt to do, they were worried. Large animals in the ocean could mean danger for swimmers. Whales might hurt swimmers in the water.

The scientists heard the warnings, and the scientists were a little afraid. But they still wanted to swim with the whales.

One scientist stood on deck by the side of the boat. She looked at the blue sea. The sky was clear and bright. The day was beautiful. And she was happy because she loved her work.

Far out in the ocean, she thought she saw something moving. The bright sun made it a little hard to see, but in seconds, she was sure. Something was moving. A whale!

"Jerome, Bob," she yelled. "I see a humpback whale!"

Jerome and Bob were scientists too. They ran to the side of the boat."

"Sonia, where is the humpback?" asked Jerome.

"Over there," said Sonia.

Bob saw it. "It is a humpback!" he said in an excited voice.

A humpback is a black-and-white whale that often lives in quiet waters. It is called a humpback because of the way its back looks when it jumps.

"We should take the boat over there to get a better look," said Sonia.

The scientists got very excited as the boat started moving closer to the whale.

"It is not just one whale; it is many whales," said Jerome.

"I count five," said Sonia.

"Me too," said Bob.

The boat went as close to the whales as the scientists thought it should for now. The captain turned off the motor and put the anchor in the water.

Sonia, Jerome, Bob, and the crew watched the five humpback whales. The whales seemed to be playing. They jumped around and made singing noises. The scientists and the crew loved the show!

"They are special animals," said Jerome.

As the scientists and the crew watched the humpback whales, they got a surprise. The whales seemed to stop playing. Then, without warning, all five whales started to swim toward the boat.

The scientists looked at each other. The captain yelled, "Sonia, the whales are moving toward us. Should I pull up the anchor and get out of here?"

Sonia looked out at the whales moving fast toward the boat.

"I don't think we can move fast enough. And I don't think we need to worry. The whales will not hurt us. We are not in danger," said Sonia.

Then she said in a soft voice only Jerome and Bob could hear, "I think."

The whales were quick. They were around the boat in no time. But they did not hit the boat. They just started to play again.

Again, the scientists and the crew just watched. No one could believe how close the whales were!

As she watched the whales, Sonia was thinking. She was one of the scientists who wanted to swim with whales. Now here were the whales. Should she change into her yellow wet suit and jump into the sea to swim with them?

The whales were very large. Sonia's guess was that each whale was about 40 feet long and as heavy as 40 tons. They were swimming very fast too. They were so fast that Sonia was not sure she could get out of their way if she was in the water with them. She did not want to get hit by 40 tons of whale tail!

Jerome knew what Sonia was thinking. "Sonia, there are tons of whales out there," he said.

"Yes, I know," said Sonia.

"Even in your yellow wet suit, you don't know if they will see you in the water," Jerome said.

"Yes, I know, but to swim with the whales is why I am here," said Sonia. Then she walked down to her cabin.

Very soon, Sonia was back on deck and dressed in her yellow wet suit and flippers.

"Jerome and Bob, I am going for a swim," she said. Jerome and Bob knew she would. Sonia was brave.

"We will go with you," said Jerome.

"Let me go alone first," said Sonia. "Jerome, will you film the whales to show how they act around me?"

"Film the whales? Sure," said Jerome.

"Bob, will you put on your wet suit and flippers and get ready to jump in after me if I get in trouble?"

"I will be back in a flash!" said Bob as he ran to put on his wet suit and flippers.

While she waited for Bob, Sonia watched the whales. As soon as Bob was back on deck, she asked, "Are ready to film, Jerome?"

"Yes, Sonia," said Jerome.

"Good!" said Sonia, and then she jumped feet first into the sea.

Sonia was in the water and swimming near the whales. She wondered if they saw her.

When she got into the middle of the whales, she started to tread water. She would tread water in this spot until she found out what the whales would do.

Sonia did not have to wait long. Almost as soon as she started to tread water, a big whale started to swim right toward her.

Sonia was afraid. She wondered what she should do. She was so small, and the humpback whale was so big. Did it even see her? Would it run right into her?

From the boat, Sonia could hear Jerome, Bob, and the crew yelling, "Look out!" They did not need to say that. She was looking out. But she could not move!

The whale was moving very fast. It came very close to Sonia, and then at the last second, it turned and went around her!

Sonia turned and watched the whale. After it passed her, it jumped into the air. Its tail hit the water far away from her.

"That was terrific," thought Sonia. The whale did see her, and it came very close. It did not hit her. It did not want to hit her! It could control its big body well. Sonia wondered if the whales were trying to learn about her as much as she was trying to learn about them.

Soon Sonia was swimming around the whales watching them play. When they rolled over, they made waves that washed over Sonia's head. The whales seemed happy Sonia was there to play with them.

Sonia learned about them as they played. She saw that whales could swim well on their backs and fronts.

The whales seemed to like each other a lot. It seemed like Sonia was in the middle of a big, happy family—a *very* big, happy family.

Jerome and Bob had seen enough. Bob jumped into the ocean, and soon he was swimming with the whales too. Jerome ran and got into his wet suit and flippers. He wanted to be part of the fun too.

When Jerome jumped in, he took his camera with him. The camera was a special one to use in water. With the camera, Jerome made a film that showed how Sonia and Bob played along with the humpback whales.

But the film Jerome made was not just any film. This film would show how whales act around each other as well as how whales act around people. Jerome would show his film to other scientists so they could learn about whales too.

Soon after Sonia, Bob, and Jerome left Hawaii and the whales, ocean scientists all over the world saw the film. That was 30 years ago. Today, because of the film, many scientists are still swimming with whales!